DIESES BUCH GEHÖRT:

[illegible]

www.ingramcontent.com/pod-product-compliance
Lightning Source LLC
Chambersburg PA
CBHW021842170526
45157CB00007B/2895
* 9 7 8 1 0 7 4 7 3 3 9 7 1 *